MW01643992

Every King Needs A Queen Love Yours

Every King Needs A Queen Love Yours

The Journey To Finding Your Perfect Mate

Troy Gloston-Phelps

ISBN: 979-8-218-10990-5

This Book is Dedicated

To all of my lovers both past and present... thank you for helping me become the man I am today.

To all of the men out there looking for their perfect mate.

And to my grandfather... Mr. Gloston

Thank You.

CHAPTERS

Introduction

As I lay back in a daze thinking of all of the ways I should start this book, my mind easily drifts to all the memories of the women from my past.

Some distant memories with fuzzy timelines, and others with details so vivid, it's as if we were just together yesterday. Yes, there are some relationships that I wish never ended, while others I wish I'd never started. But no matter how wonderful or toxic, short or long, I always learned from the relationship and took what I learned into the next. That's because dating is a process. No matter how old you are or how much the world changes, you'll learn something new. Either about yourself or about the complex thing we call relationships.

In my 32 years of being blessed to walk this Earth. I've dated teachers, strippers, singers, mothers, good girls, bad girls, etc. I've learned a lot about relationships and even more about women. Trust me when in say that no two women are the same. There may be some similarities between them, but when you get down to the details, they're as different as day and night.

I've ran into more than enough men in my life who think all women are the same and that if he treats his new woman like he did his last one, everything will be fine. They think that the relationship didn't work because there was something wrong with the woman. That she needs to be replaced like a faulty computer with a glitch in the system, or a car with a faulty part. We like to think of women as emotional, loving, caring, understanding, and perfect beings that are rolled off an assembly line. As soon as they don't fit our personal ideas of the perfect woman, we discard them like broken or defective consumer products in search of the next.

Now don't get me wrong, because not every male thinks like this. And yes, I've met women who think like this also. BUT this book is about the male aspect of relationships, written by a male. However, feel free to continue reading this if you're a woman and see some correlation in the way you or any of your female friends see relationships. I'm honored that you actually picked up this book, and opened it. So if this book helps you in any way, pass it on to a friend, no matter the gender or sexual preference.

CHAPTER 1

Relations

vs.

Relationships

(Know the Difference)

This is something new to me, even though I've been dealing with the problems that come from confusing the two since I was eighteen years young and in my first adult relationship. Let me first explain what I mean by adult relationships. I've separated all the relationships in my life into two categories, childish relationships and adult relationships.

All of my childish relationships were from my elementary, middle, and high school days—the days when I had little responsibilities and parents overseeing my life. My adult relationships started when I got a place of my own and could do as I pleased. I'm not saying that just because I was a child or in a childish relationship that I didn't love just as hard as I have in my adult relationships. What I am saying is that an adult relationship is on a totally different level of crazy and complexity.

You see, I never really understood the difference between relations and relationships. I used to think that either we were in a relationship (dating) or not. But trust me, there's a big difference in the two, and ignorance in either one CAN and probably WILL cause damage to all the parties involved—sometimes even physical damage. TRUST ME ON THIS! So to break down the differences in the two, I'll need to give you the definitions of both.

Relation, n: Connection, relationship: the state of being mutually interested or involved (as in social or commercial matters), **pl:** Dealing, affairs, sexual Intercourse

Relationship, n: the state of being interrelated.

Some people believe that both these words are the same, while others believe differently. In my personal belief, and through countless confrontations, there IS a difference between them. Let me give you one example of when confusing the two got me into a world of trouble...

There's this one girl I specifically remember. At that time in my life, she was my type: beautiful skin, pretty face, athletic body, and a cool personality. I was in my lime green Daytona Charge, looking and feeling like every other twenty-year-old male with nothing better to do than burn gas in a fast car on a beautiful day. As I was cruising by with the windows down and the music blasting, she was jogging past me in a pair of matching black and lime green athletic tights and bra. The fact that she was wearing my favorite color and matching my car was purely coincidental. I slowed down and we locked eyes. Me, at the time, having an insatiable lust for an attractive woman, slammed on the brakes and put the car in reverse. After a short conversation, we exchanged numbers, and after two weeks of texting, our paths crossed again. I needed my hair braided, and she told me that she knew how to braid hair. So I ended up at her house getting my hair braided. Well, one thing led to another, and we ended up having sex.

After we finished, there wasn't any strange or uncomfortable energy between us. It was just sex...or so I thought. About a week later, I started getting crazy text messages from her asking where I was and who I was with. I didn't think much of it until I got a call from her one night explaining to me that because we had sex, we were in a relationship. Honestly, I was confused because we'd never talked about anything remotely close to a relationship. We'd never talked about children, careers, family, futures, etc. We'd never really talked about much. So, I never gave our relationship any thought.

Most people would assume that I'd sweet-talked her out of her clothes or lied to her to get what I wanted, but it never happened like that. In the past, I've had casual sex without any strings attached, so I honestly thought that's what this was. BOY, WAS I WRONG!

I had to explain to her that there was nothing wrong with her and that the sex was amazing. It was just that I'd never put any thought into a relationship because she'd never brought it to my attention that she wanted to be in one. This was the first time that I actually paid attention to relations and relationships. It actually hurt me to hear a young, beautiful woman question herself on my behalf. To me, she didn't have any flaws, but due to confusing relations with the need for an actual relationship, I ended up hurting a woman I didn't intend to hurt.

Having relations and being in a relationship both come with great responsibility. Yes, there are women out there who see sex as just sex. But there are also women who equate sex with love and love with a relationship. So, be careful and clear about what you want. Because hurt people hurt people, and we always seem to carry our problems into our next relationship.

Now that I've talked about the differences between the two, I'd like to dig deeper on the subject of relationships.

It seems as if every living creature on Earth is looking for the perfect mate. Everything from eagles, lions, bears, and giraffes to praying mantises and crocodiles. We all go to great lengths to attract the perfect mate. Think about the clothes you wear or the way you style your hair. Yes, you may do these things because you like them, but deep down inside, it all plays a part in attracting your perfect mate.

Everything—from the way you walk to the type of cologne you wear—is an attempt to attract your perfect mate. Notice I use the word "your" in front of the words "perfect mate." Because YOUR perfect mate is exactly that: YOUR PERFECT MATE. We all have different likes and dislikes. What's perfect to me might not be perfect to you. I'm mature enough to know that no one on Earth is perfect and everyone has imperfections. But when you find your perfect mate, those imperfections will become perfect imperfections.

It's very possible to find the perfect mate, but there's one thing you'll never find: the perfect relationship. I'm sorry to disappoint, but there's no such thing as the perfect relationship. There will be arguments and disagreements. There will be ups and downs. There will be times when you question the longevity of it all. There will even be times when you look in the mirror and question yourself.

Take a look at your favorite couple—the one who looks as if they've never argued or had a disagreement. If you were to ask them, I'm pretty sure they'd tell you that they had arguments and disagreements, but that they've always managed to get back on track. To me, that's what a relationship is. It's not only about the good times, but how you made it through the rough times.

In my opinion, to survive the rough times, you'll need three basic things: SELFLESSNESS, TRUST, and HONESTY. Some of the best relationships I've been in and witnessed were successful because both partners were willing to take a lot off their mate. It's about give and take, and EVERY SUCCESSFUL RELATIONSHIP INVOLVES SELFLESSNESS! Stubbornness won't cut it.

The second quality is TRUST. Let me ask you a question...would you continue to go to a doctor you didn't trust? What if you didn't trust the car you currently drove and had enough money to buy a new car? What would you do? EXACTLY! Without trust, there's no relationship.

Last but certainly not least is HONESTY. I know it sounds simple, but the vast majority of the unsuccessful relationships I've been in and witnessed were DEAD FROM THE START! That's because the entire relationship was built on lies, or as some put it, false truths. Picture a relationship as a house. Like a house, a relationship is something that needs to be built from the ground up. Everyone will agree that the items you use to build this house will need to be strong and stable. The most important part to keeping the house strong and stable is the foundation. The foundation is the base work, and without a strong foundation, the house will fall whenever disasters come.

Let's say that disasters like wildfires, floods, and tornadoes are different troubles that attack your house (relationship). Whenever one of these disasters hits and destroys the house, all won't be lost if the foundation you laid is strong and sturdy. If so, the foundation will still be there, intact and giving you a place to rebuild. Remember, no relationship is perfect, and disasters will come.

I imagine these three qualities (selflessness/trust/honesty) as individual ropes. By themselves, they each have a certain amount of strength **BUT** if you braided all three together, you'll have a thicker and stronger rope, one that could carry more weight and tension.

Also remember that a relationship is a living and evolving thing. The further you take it, the more you'll learn from it. There isn't any sure set of rules or blueprint to a successful relationship.

This book is a set of guidelines and tools that I've personally learned throughout my life on relationships. Hopefully you'll find something in here that will help you on your journey to find the perfect mate.

CHAPTER 2

What Is Love?

(The Ultimate Question)

To me, this four-letter word is by far the most overly used and abused word in any relationship. Some people have traveled to the ends of the Earth looking for this word, while others have lived their entire lives experiencing it. Still, there are people who wouldn't know what love was if it were standing right in front of them.

Love is one of the most widely defined words of all time. Everyone has their own opinion of what love is or what it should be. I, too, used to have my own definition of the word.

So, what is love?

The Greeks defined love into four categories; 1. Agape: unselfish, unconditional, love for another, 2. Eros: erotic, relating to or dealing with sexual love, 3. Philia: love for a family member or close friend, and 4. Storgi: the love for animals.

According to Webster's dictionary, love is defined as five things; 1. Strong affection, 2. Warm attachment, 3. Attraction based on strong sexual desire, 4. A beloved person, and 5. Unselfish loyal and benevolent concern for others.

But the most complete and detailed definition of love that I've ever come across was in the Bible. It's found in 1 Corinthians 13:4-7 and states "Love is patient, love is kind. It is not jealous, pompous, inflated, or rude. It does not broad over injury and it does not rejoice over wrongdoing but rejoices with the truth. It bears all things, believes all things, endures all things."

I think everyone has used at least one of these definitions to express their love, and because love is such a powerful and complex word with so many definitions, we confuse its true meaning. There have been times in my life when I've told a woman, "I love you" based on strong sexual desire. Even though I wasn't wrong for expressing how I personally felt, some of my sexual partners felt like I was sending mixed signals. To some of them, the words "I love you" implied "I want to spend the rest of my life with you."

It got to the point where I used to think I was crazy for feeling such love based on strong sexual desire. Was I wrong to equate such wonderful and strong sexual experiences as love? No. Certainly every person who's ever felt the passionate energy like what I've experienced during sex with certain partners would agree that this amazing feeling must be love. However, no matter how justified I felt for expressing my personal feelings, I was guilty of two things: ignorance and selfishness. I say this because no matter how many different definitions there are love, the majority of people I've met define love as two categories.

1. Having love for someone.

2. Being in love with someone.

This is the great divide. This is the difference between expressing your personal feelings and selfishly ignoring the personal feelings of another. Relationships are a two-way thing, and personal perception is important. How your partner perceives the information and energy you give off is very important. There should be no guessing to whether you have love for them or are in love with them.

I remember a specific relationship that ended in chaos because I wasn't clear about which type of love I felt for my partner. I met her at a 4th of July celebration around the age of 13 or 14 and immediately fell in love with her energy. She was accompanied by a group of friends, and her aura shined as bright as a supernova in space. There was something mystic and interesting about her. Maybe it was because she was doing random cartwheels as if she was trying to master her technique. Or it might have been her smile and how goofy she was. But no matter what it was that drew me to her, I was hooked. She became my friend from that day forward, and I loved her as such.

Over the years we matured, and so did our love. But coincidentally, that was part of the problem. While my love for her as a friend matured, her love for me evolved from that of a friend into that of a mate and partner. For fifteen years, we remained friends and were never sexually intimate. That all changed in 2016, when one day she expressed her frustration with me about never giving her a chance to be my girlfriend. This kind of took me by surprise because both our lives had taken us on different paths. She was now a mother, and I was communicating with a woman I was really into. Hearing her express all the hurt she'd been enduring for the past fifteen years, seeing me dating numerous women and overlooking her, made me feel uneasy. It also made me feel guilty. It was as if I told myself that I was obligated to give her a chance, even though I'd placed her in the friend zone.

I personally have never believed in friends with benefits, so I've never mixed friendships and pleasure. It's because sex, and all the emotions that come with it, complicate things. I've always weighed the pros and cons—"Is sex worth my friendship?" and "If this doesn't work, will I lose my friend?" I've asked myself these questions numerous times in life, and not once had I ever crossed that line. But I felt obligated to her. Surely she deserved a shot, even though I only saw her as a friend. Maybe with time, I would even see her as a spouse. So I decided to go with it.

Our relationship lasted about ten months. I won't lie and say it was nonstop arguments and fighting because it wasn't. There were times when I felt at peace. Times when I was glad that we were lovers and friends. Good times. But then there were the bad times. Horrible times that seemed to suck the life and love out of us. Times that were so dark, they eclipsed and absorbed any and all light we ever shared. We both decided to go our separate ways, and even though we are still cordial, our friendship has been forever altered.

There has also been times in my life when I've felt love at first sight. And believe me, there were no mixed signals about that experience. I was stuck like a deer in headlights. Everything about me screamed, "I'm in love." This has happened to me twice, and both times it was such a strong feeling that it almost knocked me off my feet. It was as if the world had stopped spinning and time stood still. What was this I was feeling? Was it love?

In my opinion, it had to be. It felt like no other person on Earth existed. The attraction was so strong that I would've traveled to the ends of the Earth just to know this rare and beautiful creature. What I felt must have been true because in both situations, I ended up dating the female and falling in love with her. One relationship lasted three years (and thirteen years later, we're still close), and the other lasted about a year. But both ended because the relationships were lacking one or more of the qualities discussed in this book.

Do I still love the same way I did five or ten years ago? Of course not! What I've learned over the years about love is that it's like a good investment. With time, it matures into something more valuable. This is how the word "love" evolved in my life from being just a four-letter word, to Webster's definition, to what's defined in 1 Corinthians 13:4-7. It's not just a 90 or 180 degree love, but a complete 360 degree love.

But remember, before I or any of you can wholeheartedly love someone else, we need to love ourselves. Once I learned what definition of love was acceptable to me. I was able to set a standard.

CHAPTER 3

The Fab 5

(Physically, Mentally, Emotionally, Financially, Spiritually)

What I call the five aspects of a relationship have played a part in every relationship that I've ever encountered. I like to think of these aspects as a character's ability chart in a video game—that is, the speed, stamina, strength, and agility bars that read a certain number out of a max number. Like *SPEED:* 8/10, for example. Remember, there aren't any characters who come with all characteristics set at a perfect 10 out of 10.

This concept is also true in real life—no female or male is perfect in all of these aspects. As discussed earlier, there's a difference between the perfect female and your perfect female.

The perfect female doesn't exist, and you know exactly what I'm talking about. She's the one you designed in your head. The one you've pieced together using all the best parts of every woman you've ever met or dated.

SHE'S NOT REAL!

Yep, you read it right, she's not real. But let me tell you what is real: your perfect female. She might have the physical, mental, and financial aspects you like but be not as strong in the emotional and spiritual part. And that's okay, because I'm willing to bet that you're not perfect, either. But this is what makes your relationship special. This is where you'll see how compatible the two of you are. This is when you'll see how willing she is to work on those aspects you feel may need work. Just remember, it won't happen overnight. It's going to take time.

Maybe you feel like she could lose a few extra pounds or that she has poor spending habits. Or maybe she's not there emotionally. Whatever it is, just be honest and understanding with her. A relationship is all about teamwork and building towards a better future. TOGETHER! Remember, iron sharpens iron.

That being said, let's take a look at each aspect individually.

PHYSICALLY

I'm not here to body shame or make one group of women seem more special than any other group of women, but it's safe to say that we all have a type. And your type is specific to your personal interests.

For instance, I'm attracted to women with beautiful smiles. It doesn't matter what her height, weight, or skin color is. My starting point has always been the cute face with the beautiful smile. The ones who are drop-dead gorgeous naturally and don't even realize it. You, on the other hand, might be an ass man and like your women as thick as they come. Maybe you prefer women with red hair or freckles. Or do you prefer darker-toned women over lighter women?

Everyone has their own thing. I remember a guy I became cool with years ago who had a thing for plus-sized women. I remember him asking me if I knew of any big girls who were single. At first, I was caught off guard because he was a 6'9" boxer. But as it turned out, he was obsessed with plus-sized women and later married one. See, everyone is different and has a different type. Something that attracts them and is an absolute must-have in their perfect mate.

As far as aspects go, the physical is one of the most complicated aspects because it's not easy to change. For example, if you're dating a woman who's five feet tall but you like women who are at least six feet tall, it's certainly going to be hard to change that aspect of her. So, for the most part, what you see is what you get.

However, there have been times when I've seen women who feel the need to alter their physical appearance. Take, for example, a woman who breast-fed her children and wants to get her breasts lifted. Or a woman who wants to get her butt done. Be sure that you can live with whatever physical changes your woman desires.

We are all human, and as humans, we judge ourselves harder than others do. And women are no different. I know beautiful women who have beaten themselves down because of their self-consciousness and lack of attention from their mate.

So don't be a dick! ALWAYS LET THE WOMAN IN YOUR LIFE KNOW HOW BEAUTIFUL SHE IS!

MENTALLY

Who doesn't like an educated women? What about both book smart and street smart? Everyone has a certain intellectual level they go for. I've never dated a nuclear physicist, and I'm not saying that I couldn't, either, but I don't know anything about nuclear science. So, how far do you think we could go before my simple education is exhausted and I can no longer mentally stimulate her?

Notice I said "mentally stimulate." This works for not only women but men as well. Have you ever dated someone who didn't mentally stimulate you? I have, and it was like being trapped in a padded room. The conversations were boring and bland. It was as if we had nothing in common. For instance, what if you like sci-fi movies and attending sci-fi events, and your partner doesn't care for them at all? You'd start to feel as if what you're interested in is unimportant, and eventually the connection would fail.

I once dated a woman who was interested in ancient beings and ancient alien secrets. Even though I'd never been into it as much as she was. I was open to learning. So, during the time when I'd usually put on an action movie, I decided to watch documentaries on underwater pyramids and ancient aliens. For starters, I learned a few things. Second, it wasn't as bad as I thought it would be. And lastly, but most importantly, I made her feel comfortable with the things she was interested in. Remember, this works both ways.

For instance, I'm a very big car guy and I remember how she had zero car knowledge. She didn't know the difference between a V12 and a V8, or the difference between a Porsche and Lamborghini. But what used to make me feel good was that I would catch her putting on car shows and actually watching them. What made it even more special was that throughout the shows, she'd ask me questions about what we were watching. The fact that she wanted to connect with me through things that interested me was a big turn-on.

EMOTIONALLY

How many of you have ever dated a crazy person? I'm pretty sure we've all dated a woman with crazy tendencies, and if you haven't, YOU'RE TRULY BLESSED. I remember dating a female who was in a few bad relationships before she got with me. She'd been abused, used, and cheated on—all of which left her an emotional wreck. She'd be happy one second, and extremely sad the next. No matter how loyal and honest I was with her, she always thought I was cheating.

To make matters worse, when we'd argue, the arguments would become heated. So heated, she would physically attack me. I've never been the type of guy to physically abuse my partner, nor am I the one who accepts physical abuse. There's a saying, "If I got to beat you, then I don't need you." I realized that she wasn't emotionally strong enough to be in a relationship, and we only lasted six months.

As a male, I constantly remind myself that females are more in touch with their emotions and I need to dial into my sensitive side to get understanding sometimes. As males, we, or some of us, were raised to hide our emotions. We were told to toughen up. But I've learned that there's nothing wrong with being in touch with your emotional side and that it's good to soften things up sometimes. Some of the things I used to never care about, I now emphasize with. I try to see things from her point of view. I try to see things from her point of view.

Remember, FOR EVERY ACTION, THERE IS A REACTION. If your mate is being emotional, there has to be a reason. Sometimes she may just need a hug or for you to tell her how beautiful she is. Other times, it might be stress from work or parenthood. But no matter what it is, it's YOUR job to be there for her emotionally. Remember to be her calm in whatever storm she's going through.

FINANCIALLY

How many times have you dreamed of dating a rich woman? Yeah, I know, but you're not the only one. Wanting someone who's more than financially stable isn't a crime. It doesn't mean you're shallow or a gold digger; it just means that you'd like to be with a woman who's about her business, and there's nothing wrong with that. The only problem I have with that is when her money becomes your main focal point.

For ages, I've watched TV shows, movies, and other people telling young women to date lawyers, doctors, and businessmen. As I matured, I realized that this was the wrong attitude to have—it's the same as saying DON'T date teachers, garbage men, or anyone who makes a certain amount of income. I've seen how this statement tips the scales in relationships. It makes it harder on men and tends to mislead a lot of women into wanting a guy based on his bank account, and not his natural worth.

I think that's why as a society, we tend to think of females as gold diggers more than males. But as we all know, men can be gold diggers as well. My point is that you don't like someone solely based on their money. Your relationship will never last, and you'll both be unhappy with each other. You shouldn't base your love on someone's income, and you should never try to buy someone's love with your income. Not everyone wants the Bentley, mansion, and yacht. There are a lot of men who make the mistake of putting their focus on making money for the relationship and forget about the relationship. They end up replacing emotional support, physical presence, and time with expensive gifts that hold no value.

Let me ask you a question...how many relationships have you seen end and both of the people involved were financially stable? See what I'm saying!

I know a lot of people who are deeply in love and aren't rich. We all know the saying, "More money, more problems." So if you do happen to be dating a woman who's wealthy, remember to keep your focus on her and not her money. Making less than her doesn't make you less of a man. Trying to shower her with lavish trips and expensive things probably won't cut it, because she's financially stable enough to do all of that on her own. Remember, she's attracted to you for the things she can't do on her own!

SPIRITUALLY

Sadly, this is one of the most overlooked and neglected aspects of a relationship. There are roughly 8 billion people on the planet Earth, and no two are the same. There are specific religions and beliefs we all have that play key roles in our relationships. Most of the time, we are born into these religions or beliefs, and they have stuck with us over the years. As humans, we tend to date within those religious or spiritual beliefs. However, there might come a time when your heart leads you to someone who isn't of the same religious or spiritual beliefs as you.

I remember dating this beautiful woman who didn't believe in Jesus Christ as I do. She wasn't disrespectful or argumentative, and I wasn't pushy or demanding about the topic. I just let her know that I'd love for her to experience church with me and that it would strengthen our relationship. Eventually, she started to go with me to church and share in my spiritual experiences.

Now let me be clear...I'm not saying that because I'm a Christian, my relationships will work out. That would be crazy to think. I have a friend who's Muslim and his relationships are just as complicated as mine. So no, your spiritual and religious beliefs won't be the underlying factor in determining if your relationship works out. But they will play a part. So find out what she believes in and be open-minded. Just because you're the "man" in the relationship doesn't mean she should conform to your ways.

CHAPTER 4

SEX!

(Confusion, Chaos, Pleasure)

Originally, I wanted to include this section in the "FAB 5" section, but sex deserves its own chapter altogether. It's the one aspect of any relationship that holds all the others in limbo. It's so strong, it's the only aspect we continually confuse with love. It's as if sex overrides all of the other aspects.

Disagree? Well, have you ever had sex with a woman who wasn't financially stable or physically to your liking? What about sex with a woman who wasn't on the same page as you spiritually? I have.

Let me ask you a simple question...what if you were dating a woman who was financially, mentally, emotionally, spiritually, and physically to your liking? She had everything you could ask for, BUT the sex was horrible. I'm talking, no arousal or excitement at all. How long would the relationship last before you were to leave or cheat? See my point?

On the other hand, what if she was broke, crazy, and not your type physically but the sex was amazing? Would you continue to pursue your sexual desires with her? I thought so. No, you're not crazy or some shallow sexual monster. You're just like the rest of us who enjoy great sex.

Sadly, there are some people who might not know what I mean when I say "great Sex." So let me give you an idea of what I'm talking about. It's an out of body experience. It's almost like a game of war between the individuals involved, as if each one is trying to conquer the other with concentrated amounts of passion. It's as if time stops. It's primal. It's as if there's nothing holding you back. It feels as if you just hit the lotto or turned into some talented bedroom hero. When it's good, you can feel the energy being transferred from one body to another.

Great sex is patient and mystic. It feels as if you're on the edge of the highest cliff, and then you fall into ecstasy and drown in pleasure. When it's good, it's the one aspect in a relationship where you can be you in the rawest form. There's something about the nakedness that makes us feel fragile and empowered at the same time.

I remember when I first explored sex. I was fifteen and didn't know what I was doing. The girl I was with was more experienced than I was, and now as I look back on that experience, I laugh at how inexperienced I was. Since then, I've advanced in ways I can't explain. I've learned that sex isn't so much about "getting me" but giving my partner a personal experience.

Most of the men I've talked to don't seem to realize that sex is a three-part experience. It's physical, mental, and emotional. It's not just about pounding and slapping ass. It's way deeper.

For starters, if a woman is willing to let you have sex with her, then she's letting you into her world. So, be RESPECTFUL! She might be the most beautiful woman in your eyes, but trust me, her mind's moving a thousand miles a minute. Every woman has her own personal insecurities. She might feel as if her breasts aren't big enough, or her oral skills aren't the best. That's when you should compliment her on how perfect her breasts are or how her oral skills drive you crazy.

Also, get to know your woman. Find out what she likes and dislikes. You should always make her feel comfortable. I know some women who seem so innocent in public, but in bed, they turn into a sexual goddess. Everyone has a fetish, so keep that in mind. I've met women who love anal but have been too afraid to tell men because they're afraid of being judged. THIS IS A PROBLEM AND IT NEEDS TO STOP! There shouldn't be double standards when it comes to sex. Just because she's sure of herself sexually doesn't mean she's a slut or a ho. We are all different and have different arousals.

Take me for example. I love, love, love giving oral sex. And I've been in a relationship with a woman who didn't feel comfortable being eaten out because of past experiences. But it was my job to make her feel comfortable. I enjoy it when a woman tells me that she's turned on by a new experience or that she never knew she'd like a certain thing we tried. But remember, in order to unlock great sex with your partner, there needs to be TRUST! When she trusts you, she'll relax and feel comfortable. When she's comfortable with you, she'll feel free to be herself and open up sexually.

Without that connection, you'll never have great sex. So, take your time and experience everything that sex has to offer. Start with her feet and work your way up to her head. Keep in mind that you should always be honest with all your sexual partners. Sex should never be used as leverage to get what you want or to control someone. I've seen the type of damage this attitude has caused many women. Always remember that with great power comes great responsibility.

Let's say that you're one of the many men who aren't advanced sexually and haven't had much experience when it comes to pleasing a woman. Not to worry. Sex, like anything else on Earth, gets better with two things: knowledge and practice. Practice makes perfect! The more you try it, the more comfortable you'll become with it. Second, knowledge is power! There are plenty of sexual self-help books out there that explore everything from oral to anal and techniques to positions. No matter what comes your way sexually, there's a book to help you out.

CHAPTER 5

Know Yourself, Know Your Partner

(Let's be REAL)

How well do you know yourself? This seems like a dumb question, right? Because the majority of us know our likes and dislikes. But that's not the problem. The problem is, "Are you being honest with yourself?"

For a long time, in many of my relationships, I would ignore myself. Things that I knew would end up being a problem eventually became BIG PROBLEMS, and that was all because I was being dishonest with myself.

Let me give you a few examples of what I mean. I used to date a female who smoked cigarettes. I'm not a smoker, so of course I didn't like the smell of them. And she smoked everywhere—in the car, in the house, and even on dates. It affected us physically. Eventually, she noticed the distance and called me out on it. I explained to her why I was so distant and the negative effects cigarettes have on people. To my surprise, she looked at me and replied, "Why haven't you been told me this? I would've tried to quit a long time ago." This was love. Within a year, and with thorough dedication and hard work, she kicked the habit.

See what I mean about being honest and upfront? I was letting something I didn't like affect my entire relationship. It turns out that most people are willing to give up a few things for the betterment of their relationship, especially when those things are bad habits. Still, there are times when you end up with a stubborn partner, and small problems that are left unchecked turn into relationship-ending problems.

I once had a male friend who was dating a woman who worked for a big hotel franchise. She was a manager and her boss (a general manager) was a bit of a flirt. For some time, my friend would ignore the flirting that her boss would throw her way. But eventually, he brought it to my attention and I told him to tell his female partner about it. He looked at me as if I'd told him to jump off the Eiffel Tower. He explained to me that he didn't want to seem like a paranoid or insecure boyfriend. THIS is another problem with us men! We hate to seem vulnerable or insecure. It's not always a good thing, BUT we are human beings and there will come a time when all of us have to put our pride to the side. This is also why communication is so important.

You have to be able to relay how you feel and why you feel this particular way. Remember that communication is both verbal and nonverbal. So, watch what you say and how you say it. It's okay to be honest. Just remember that there is a time and place for everything.

For instance, I remember a time when a woman I was dating had went out and got her hair done in a style I thought looked horrible. When I first caught sight of her sporting this new hairstyle, I immediately froze in place. Here she was, staring at me and smiling from ear to ear, and I'm just looking at her in shock. After a few seconds of awkward silence, her smile faded and she asked, "You don't like it?" My honest and insensitive reply was, "No, I don't like it. What made you do this?" As you can probably tell, this conversation didn't turn out well. It wasn't because I was being honest; it was because in the process of being honest, I was also being insensitive, and not just verbally, but nonverbally.

My physical (nonverbal) reaction to her told her I didn't like her hairstyle way before I actually said anything. This is what I learned to work on. Let me give you a quick example of how I'd handle that same conversation now while still being honest and understanding of her feelings.

She pops up sporting her new hairdo. My reaction: "I see that you got a new hairstyle." Her reply: "Do you like it?" I reply: 'It's okay, but I really like the (fill in the blank with your favorite hairstyle) because I think it compliments your (fill in the blank) more."

But remember, it's all about HOW you say it! This helps in any situation. There might come a time when you're asked THE HARDEST QUESTION OF THEM ALL—"Honey, do you think I'm fat?" After this question, the next few seconds will be some of the most important seconds of your relationship. It can either go one way or the other.

If you honestly feel like she hasn't gained any weight, then your answer is simple: "Hell, no, sweetheart you look good!" But if you honestly feel like she's gained a few unwanted pounds, then you'd better say something on the lines of this: "No, sweetheart, I don't think that you're fat. If anything, it's me who's gained a few pounds and I've been wanting to hit the gym. If you feel like you need to lose a few pounds, maybe we can go together?"

Remember, it's all about how you say it, so loosen up and smile a bit. Let her know that no matter what, you love her and are deeply attracted to her.

Knowing yourself just doesn't mean how you interact with your partner, but also how you control yourself. Awhile back, I had an instructor who explained to me how he used to set personal road blocks to keep him from making poor decisions. He's married with three kids, and his wife's job is one that consists of traveling for a few days out of the month. He said that instead of sending the kids off to be with their grandparents and being alone, he keeps the children while his wife is gone. When I asked him why, he explained, "It's simple—if my wife is away in another part of the country and my children are at their grandparents, I'll have nothing better to do than get into trouble. So instead of me sending the children off for two or three days. I keep them home with me as a reminder of all the things I love and care for. Plus, I get to build a stronger bond with my children and my wife loves it."

Do you see how because my instructor knows himself, he's able to set boundaries in his life? Now this might not be you. Maybe you can spend three days alone and not mess up, but everyone's different and the goal is to KNOW YOURSELF!

CHAPTER 6

Nobody's Perfect

(WE ALL HAVE FAULTS)

To my understanding, theres only been one person to walk the Earth and be perfect: JESUS! So if you're looking for someone who's perfect, I suggest you open a Bible.

There's no such thing as the perfect female; there is only your perfect female. Understand the difference? Using one specific woman as a bottom line or score sheet for all other women is not only unfair but ridiculous! Comparing every female in your life to this one person is insane.

Maybe it was a created woman (like the woman of your dreams). You know the one I'm talking about—the one with every single positive trait you like in a woman, and none of the negatives. GET REAL! She doesn't exist. If you're judging every woman based on your idea of the perfect woman, you'll never be satisfied. Think about if the shoe was on the other foot? Do you really believe that you're the perfect man? Exactly! I didn't think so. And if you think that you're the perfect man, do me a favor... close this book and give it to someone who's not a self-centered jerk.

NOBODY'S PERFECT! We all have imperfections. We all have a past. We, as men, sometimes seem to forget this. We forget when we lied or cheated. We forget when we weren't good listeners or good sexual partners. We always seem to forget when we failed as relational partners. When we forget or ignore our own faults, we think of ourselves more highly then we should, which is why we are so judgmental of our partners. We're searching for that special woman to mirror the false perception of our perfect selves.

To me, there are only two types of people on planet Earth: those who see the glass as half-empty, and those who see it as half-full. You see, if you're always looking at your partner as less then, you'll never be happy. If you focus on her faults more than her positives, you'll never be happy. I'm not saying to ignore their shortcomings; what I am saying is that nobody's perfect. If you are one of those perfectionists who tend to spend more time detailing someone's imperfections and faults more than their positive attributes, you'll never be happy! No matter who you date or how perfect she is, you'll never be satisfied. As long as you focus on their shortcomings, you'll never see the positives.

No relationship partner can change this. This is a problem within yourself and needs to be dealt with first, or your relationship will never bring you happiness. Optimism and sacrificing go hand and hand. In order to see the best in someone, you'll need to sacrifice some of your personal concepts and wants. In other words, you'll need to "give and take." This is a fundamental key to any relationship on Earth.

Whether it's a trade deal between two countries or a symbiotic relationship between ants and a tree, what we give and take plays a part. Once you understand that concept, you'll understand sacrifices and imperfections.

For the most part, the majority of men I've came across understand that nobody's perfect. This isn't their problem; their problem is one I used to have. I like to call it I.N.T.B. (It's Not That Bad).

It's when you take something small and blow it out of proportion. Let me give you an example of a time when I had an I.N.T.B. moment.

One Sunday morning, I woke up to the smell of a wonderful breakfast being cooked by a beautiful woman I was dating. As I made my way to the kitchen, I noticed that she had taken it upon herself to clean my place. Everything was neat and organized. As I sat down on the couch, she delivered my breakfast with a kiss. While we were eating breakfast, the buzzer from my washing machine sounded, and she made the comment that my clothes must be finished. I instantly looked to the spot where I'd left my $1,200 denim jeans lying the night before. They weren't there. My stomach instantly dropped as I rushed to the laundry room. When I opened the washing machine, not only did I find my light blue Balmain jeans but I also noticed my black Balmain jeans. Right then and there, I lost it! So now, I'm ranting and raving about how you're not supposed to machine-wash these expensive jeans, let alone wash the light blue with the black.

Now the entire time that I'm going off (about five minutes), she's sitting on the couch quietly eating her breakfast. When I finally stopped to get her feedback, she very patiently and politely asked me, "Are you finished?" I was caught off-guard by how calm she was and I ended up just staring at her. Realizing that I was at a loss for words, she said to me, "So let me get this straight. You woke up to a wonderful breakfast, cooked by a beautiful woman, who also decided to clean your place...and you're upset because she washed your clothes?"

Damn...she had me right. I couldn't even move, let alone say anything. She stood up and walked over to my frozen body, gave me a kiss that instantly melted me, and then hung my jeans on the balcony to dry.

You see what I mean about I.N.T.B.? I was taking something small and turning it into something big. I had to remember that she, like me, wasn't perfect. We were the same in some ways, but different in others. One way that we were different was that I was into high fashion and she wasn't. She didn't know the difference between Balmain and Levis, nor did she care. Was this a fault? No! I could never fault her because I was a slave to big-named designers. As a matter of fact, I was more attracted to her for being an inexpensive fashionista versus a label goddess.

I try to use everyday situations like this to shine a light on my imperfections. This situation showed me how quick-tempered and caught up in myself I was. We all have I.N.T.B. moments—the point is knowing the difference. Maybe the woman you're involved with has trust issues. When you go out with friends, she may tend to text or call just a little more than you may like. NOBODY'S PERFECT! Instead of creating a I.N.T.B. moment by feeling she doesn't trust you, flip the optimism switch on and see it as though she misses you and wants to make sure you're okay.

I bet if your attitude towards her is positive, slowly but surely, she'll ease up on all the calls and text messages. YOUR ATTITUDE PLAYS A PART! If you're defensive, chances are she'll think that you're trying to hide something. Try to understand that, just like you, she has a past. Remember that sometimes our past will get the best of us. Nobody's perfect and we all have faults.

CHAPTER 7

Stereotypes

(Believing in Their Truth, You'll Live a Life of Lies)

Who hasn't heard of a stereotype concerning any specific type of woman? Chances are, you've probably heard hundreds. Stereotypes are everywhere. Everyone who's anyone has some sort of stereotype they believe in. Some stereotypes are self-hypothesized while others have been passed to us from family and friends. Some stereotypes might even be harmless, while others hurt to the core.

When it all boils down to it, stereotypes are just our assumptions and opinions of a specific type of woman. Let's be honest—we're all guilty of either spreading our stereotypes or letting them rule us. Being a male of thirty-two years. I've heard all sorts of stereotypes. These are just a few:

"Financially secure and independent women are too busy and hard to please."

"Highly educated women are innocent (good girls) while strippers are more sexually active (bad girls)."

"Thicker women get extremely wet and skinny women can take more."

"Women with expensive taste are gold diggers and women with children have too many problems to deal with."

The list goes on and on. We've all formulated some sort of stereotype from past experiences or opinions of women, but none should be taken seriously. Each and every individual woman is different.

I've personally dated a woman who was stripping at the time. Our relationship lasted three years and she was one of the most beautiful, mature, and complex women I've ever dated. She was also well-mannered and highly educated. No one ever expected her to be a stripper. That's because stripping wasn't who she was as a person. Being a stripper was just one small subdivision of her.

I also dated a plus-sized woman who graduated college with a degree in biological engineering. Our relationship lasted about four years on and off, and was by far one of the worst relationships I've ever been in. She was a compulsive liar as well as a cheater. To make matters worse, she stole a significant amount of money from me. If stereotypes were true, she was supposed to be the exact opposite of what she actually was.

I also remember having this female GM at a job I used to work at. Everyone was afraid of her. She was always serious and never really laughed at anything. We ended up throwing a party for one of our coworkers and this GM showed up. We all thought that the person we knew from the job would be the same one at the party. Boy, were we wrong! She turned out to be the life of the party.

You see, every environment and situation is different. Our problem is that we stereotype an entire category of women based on the actions of a few. This is ignorant, disrespectful, and downright dangerous. There are even stereotypes that are racially motivated. As a black male, I've heard a lot of my fellow black men say, "White women are more loyal than black women" or "White women are more open-minded sexually than black women." These, like other racially charged stereotypes are untrue, personally opinionated, and highly offensive. I've been blessed to date both black and white women—notice I said 'women,' plural. So, trust me when I say that race holds no merit to the honesty, integrity, sexual desire, loyalty, or intellect of a woman.

Most of the men I hear speaking of these stereotypes have rarely or never dated outside of their race. They're just repeating the opinions of what they've heard or read. To me, stereotypes are the biggest road blocks in finding the perfect mate. There are a lot of good women who are single because they've been stereotyped and categorized for things they haven't done. Think of all the hard-working single mothers or powerful business women. What about the quiet, down-to-earth women, or the outgoing independent women? Every woman deserves a chance, free of prejudgment and stereotypes

CHAPTER 8

Beauty's in the Eye of the Beholder

(What Are You Attracted To?)

Just like automobiles, jewelry, and artwork, every female has something special about them that catches your eye. So let me ask you a personal question, one that only you can answer...what do you like in a woman? Everyone has their own thing.

Next time you're around a group of guys, ask each of them what they're attracted to. I'm sure that you'll hear a variety of things.

Some will say lips and others might say eyes. Some will say ass while others argue breasts. When I sit back and think of what I'm attracted to the most, it's got to be the face. I love a beautiful face—somewhat mystic with a little hint of attitude. Innocent yet mischievous. A face with a future and a past. This is what catches my attention. I won't lie and say that everything else holds no value; that would be untruthful. I just always start with the face, and the face is just the beginning.

I've dated all tones on the color spectrum, but I find myself attracted to women of color the most—everything from chocolate to the color of honey. And I love it when women rock their hair somewhat natural. I honestly don't even know the exact name of the hairstyle, but it reminds me of a lion's mane. An example is the way Tracey Ellis Ross wears her hair.

You see, these are the things that I find attractive. And no, this isn't a complete list because that would take an entire book.

I'm not saying, "If she doesn't look like 'this,' she isn't beautiful." We all have a type, even if that type continuously changes. What I might find unattractive, you may go crazy for. Hence the saying, 'One man's trash is another man's treasure." You have to learn what turns you on. But remember, beauty is deeper than just appearance.

To me, a woman's attitude is just as attractive. The way she walks into a room and commands attention, or how she handles adversity—all of which plays a role in how attracted I am to her. And remember that we all age (except J.Lo and Pharrell). So with that being understood, we won't look the same at fifty as we do at twenty-five. But true beauty never ages. Once you find your perfect mate, that undistinguishable fire will never diminish but grow hotter over time.

CHAPTER 9

The Breadwinner

(Who Wears the Pants?)

Are you the man of the house? Seems like a stupid question, but there are a lot of men who ask themselves this question every day.

But to answer this question, you must first know what it means to be "the man of the house." Now, I can only give you my opinion of this. It's a mixture of things I've experienced and was taught. To be the man of the house doesn't mean that you have to make more money than your spouse/girlfriend. It doesn't mean that you have to go out and work while your spouse/girlfriend stays home. It doesn't even mean that you have to bear all the weight or make all the important decisions.

I think the old way of how we saw being the man of the house has crippled some of us, especially with how our society is today. Gone are the days when it was frowned upon for the male figure to stay at home and watch the children or cook and clean while the woman goes to work. To me, being the man of the house has transformed from a physical aspect to more of a mental one. Being the man of the house in a mental aspect is even more important to our society than a physical one. Just think about it.

We like to think of the man of the house as the breadwinner, the one who makes the money. This is a caveman's way of thinking. Sure, way back then, the men used to go out and hunt for the food while the women and children stayed home. It was all genetics back then. Genetically speaking, men are physically stronger than women, and women possess the power to bring forth life. So of course, men went out to hunt. But this is the 21st century, not the Ice Age.

There are a lot of women who are more than capable enough of putting food on the table. I think this is the reason why there are so many independently and financially stable single women out there today—it's because a lot of men feel uncomfortable with a partner that makes more than them. For some reason, it makes them feel less than or inferior. We, as men, have to remember that being the man of the house is about being a good leader. And a few characteristics of a good leader are: honor, integrity, selflessness, and courage . In JROTC., I learned that a good leader was also a great follower.

Don't get so caught up in this manly man thing that you mess up something good. Would you jeopardize your spouse/girlfriend's career because she makes more than you? What if it meant you had to stay home and watch the kids? Would you let your insecurities effect the peace in your relationship? I hope not. Remember, money isn't everything. How many men do you know with plenty of money (big money) and still have multiple divorces?

See, there's more to being the man of the house than just money. But if you are one of those men who's been blessed to have a woman that's a hard worker and makes more than you, do me a favor. First, thank GOD. Then, tell her how lucky you are to have her in your life.

CHAPTER 10

Cheaters/Cheating

(The End of Relationships)

Yes, I said it—CHEATING! The number-one cause for tragedy and turmoil in any relationship.

How many of us have been guilty of cheating? Why do so many of us cheat? Can a relationship survive the ultimate betrayal? Once a cheater, always a cheater? There are many questions when it comes to cheating, but to find answers, you must first look at the problem.

So, what is cheating? By definition, the word "cheat" means. **1. To deprive of something through fraud or deceit, 2. To violate rules dishonestly, and 3. To be sexually unfaithful.** Fraud, deceit, dishonesty, and unfaithfulness...all of these words describe cheating.

If you've ever cheated, chances are you've felt like one of these words. Yes, I might have cheated, but I'm not a cheater.

There's a bit of a lesson you learn as you mature. It has to do with love. Seeing the hurt and destruction I caused someone I was supposed to love changed everything for me. But before I get into this story, I need to take you to a time prior. Before my adult relations and before things were so complex. Let me take you back to when I was only a freshman in high school.

I was the new kid attending Nile C. Kinnick High School and was madly in love with the daughter of a pastor. She had this fire about herself. Her attitude and spice was intoxicating to me. I was hooked and used to do all the things any love-drunk adolescent in high school would. I'd carry her books, walk her to class, and eat lunch with her. I took pride in being a gentleman. I thought I was everything she needed. But boy, was I wrong! You see, when you're an adolescent, there's this thing called sex. It's something you hear about, and is mostly treated like taboo. But once you've experienced it, there's no turning back. It's as if the world has new meaning. There's now this new uncontrollable itch that needs scratching. I, at the time, was blind to sex because I was still a virgin, but to my ignorance, she wasn't. She had tasted pleasure.

Early in our relationship, I started to notice things. I'd notice that my girlfriend would be late for lunch sometimes or I'd miss her after classes. One afternoon, I caught her and this senior coming back to the school campus. He rode the same bus as me and was the definition of a basketball jock. A pretty boy with swagger for days.

Her initial reaction was shock, but his was cool and collected. He gave her a hug and went towards the bus. She walked up to me, said that she'd call me later, and with a hug and a kiss she went to catch her bus. Well, I didn't really think too much of it because remember, I was green as baby shit and hadn't experienced sex.

While on the bus ride home, a female junior made the comment to me, "You okay with that?" She was pointing towards the jock. I looked at her kind of lost, but replied, "Yeah, they're good friends." It was as if the entire bus started laughing at me. The female junior replied,

"Friends? Everybody knows that your girlfriend's a little ho!" I looked at the jock who had this smug look on his face, and my stomach instantly turned into an EF5 tornado. It seemed as if everyone knew about this but me.

That night, I ignored all her calls and tried to distance myself from her at school. But two days later she confronted me and I asked her what I'd already known. She broke down crying and explained how sorry she was. She made it seem like she couldn't explain why she was doing it, like her body couldn't be controlled. But all other things she explained to me, I couldn't comprehend at the time. It all made no sense, and there were two reasons why. First, I wasn't a cheater, and second, I'd never experienced sex.

But let me tell you, the hurt and pain she caused me stayed with me like a stigma. Like some sort of curse. There it was, a tiny seed planted inside of me, growing and growing over the years. Our relationship was forever changed after that day. She ended up being the first female I had sex with, and throughout the rest of my high school years, we continued to remain sexual. But no matter how much I wanted to tell her, I loved her, I couldn't. I wouldn't. I didn't. I used her for one thing: sex.

By my sophomore year, I'd become the captain of our top-ranked football team and was getting a lot of attention from other females. She, on the other hand, didn't play any sports or participate in any school teams. I would see her in the hallways and ignore her, as if we hadn't just had sex or were going to have sex.

One day after one of our sexual events, she cried and asked me why we couldn't be in a relationship. She apologized over and over for what she did and told me that she loved me. The sad part was that I believed her.

I knew that she loved me, and without any doubt in my mind, I loved her. But I could never say it to her. I could never open up myself to be hurt like that again. So I said what any hurt, broken-hearted, soulless boy would say. I told her that she would never have my heart again and that sex would be the only part of me she would be able to have. As I looked into her eyes, I saw the hurt and pain I felt the day on that school bus my freshman year.

As I think about it now, I feel terrible and owe her an apology. I was young, petty, and ignorant back then. Besides, hurt people hurt people. But like I said, the results of her unfaithfulness plagued me for years and years afterwards. I felt like cheaters and cheating were beneath me. Boy, was I wrong!

The year was 2007. I was nineteen years young and about six months into a relationship with a wonderful woman six years my senior. This was also my first adult relationship living with a partner. Everything was perfect until I got into a few legal battles that cost me a lot. Money started to get tight, and our lifestyle started to change. There were no more weekend shopping sprees or expensive dinners. I even lost my car, a Mercedes E-class. Even though she didn't seem to mind or treat me any differently because of our new financial shortcomings, I felt less than.

I felt less than a man. I let my pride take control. I used to be the man with the nice car that supplied every financial need for my woman. Now, I was the man who could barely keep the lights on. I held her up on this throne and felt as though without all of the money, I wasn't worthy of having her.

So my energy towards her was off. I wasn't my usual self and I was giving off bad vibes. I was short-tempered and easily aggravated. I was creating an emptiness between us, and in turn, she started to distance herself.

I was the one pushing her away, but I didn't see it like that. There was a female I'd met while being out and about one day, and we were getting closer. My girlfriend wasn't giving me much attention, and I did what a lot of men do who don't feel as though they are getting the attention they need: I cheated on my girlfriend with a female who was giving me a lot of attention.

I still can't completely explain the feeling. There's something embedded in between the excitement and fear of getting caught. It's like stealing a forbidden fruit. It's not supposed to feel good, but it does, it most definitely does. It was as if I wasn't conscious at all; I was only focused on the task at hand. During our interaction, I felt empowered, I felt important, and most importantly, I felt needed again.

But the worse part about cheating (as far as issues go) is the feeling you have afterwards. As soon as I was finished, I was back to reality ,and I felt like shit. All the powerful, exciting feelings and emotions I experienced, I immediately wanted to erase. I wanted to reverse time. If you've ever cheated on someone you've loved and have never felt like this, then chances are you didn't love them or you're a psychopath.

The hardest part is going back to your girlfriend and trying to act normal. But sadly, I learned to control this behavior with practice. That was the first time I ever cheated, but it wasn't the last. I didn't get caught that time, but throughout out our three-year relationship, I got caught plenty of times afterwards. It was as if I had a sickness or new addiction. No matter how bad I felt or how much I was hurting my girlfriend, I couldn't stop. Now I finally understood what my ex had been going through all those years ago.

You see, most people believe that when men cheat, it's all physical, and when women cheat, it's emotional. Well, I can tell you that's a lie. Yes, there have been times when I've cheated and felt no type of wanting for the female. But the majority of the time, I was deeply attracted to the woman I was cheating with. It wasn't just a physical attraction but an emotional one. Here lies another problem.

When you cheat, you're not just hurting the woman you're cheating on. You're also hurting the woman you're cheating with. Especially when feelings get involved. Trust me on this. I've been in this situation plenty of times before, and I end up stuck between a rock and a hard place—in love with two women who have strengths were the other lacks. It's a toxic situation that destroys women all over the globe. It leaves each woman asking herself, "What's wrong with me? Am I not enough?" It leaves this lasting emotional scar that makes them second-guess their worth. It has literally turned beautiful, self-confident women into bitter, self-conscious ones. You see, when you cheat, you break trust, and trust is the foundation of any and every relationship. When you encounter women with trust issues, the majority of the time, this is why. It's an ongoing cycle of hurt that gets carried into future relationships.

It wasn't until one summer night in 2009 that I learned my lesson. The love of my life—my girlfriend of three years—decided to sleep with a mother man. She did it as a "fuck you" to me, as payback for all of the times I betrayed her. She didn't even try to hide it; she wanted me to know what she'd done.

My world instantly came crashing down around me. I hated her. I hated myself. I hated everything. I was numb and everything seemed bland. She had brought me all the way back to that day when I was a freshman in high school. All of those memories of hurt and pain hit me at once.

I wanted to die, and part of me did. That was the last day we were together. Even though we've remained close all these years, we've never crossed that line again. She still apologizes for what happened as if it were her fault we didn't make it. The fault was all mine...**I** didn't man up...**I** wasn't a good leader or follower...**I** forced her to cheat. **I** forced her into another man's bed.

The sad part is that I see this same pattern with a lot of relationships. The man will cheat and the woman will forgive him continuously. But when the woman cheats, it's over.

In my honest opinion. I believe the reason for this is because as men, we are prideful creatures. We are like powerful locomotives powered by pride instead of coal. Sometimes, more often than not, we let our pride get in the way of our true feelings, which is what drives our unfair way of thinking. Our excuse has become our reason. We use the excuse that we are men as our reason to cheat, as if it's part of our genetic code. This is biased and sexist, though I once used to be fooled by this misconception. There are a lot of people who believe it isn't okay to cheat, but, if a man does it, it was understandable. Yet, if a woman were to cheat, it's unforgivable.

So years ago, if you were to ask me, "Does cheating ruin a relationship?", I would've answered yes. I would have said, "Yes, because cheating destroys trust and that trust can never be rebuilt." But as I've matured and experienced more relationships. I would now answer 'no', cheating isn't the end-all to a relationship. I've seen relationships that are thriving healthy and strong, even though one or both of the partners have cheated. Not only have I witnessed this, but a few years ago, I was in a relationship where a female cheated on me and I forgave her. I wasn't petty or bitter. I didn't treat her like a whore or a prostitute. I didn't beat her or put her down.

I just looked into my own past and remembered all the times I've cheated. No, I'm not saying that it's okay to accept being cheated on. No, I'm not saying that it's going to be easy forgiving them, either. What I am saying is that no one's perfect, male or female, and love (as defined in 1 Cor 13) is forgiving and without contempt. So yes, cheating hurts, but you must ask yourself, "Is this relationship worth fighting for?"

CHAPTER 11

The Ex

(What They Mean to Us and the Connections We Share)

You never forget an ex, no matter how long or short the relationship. It doesn't matter if the relationship was toxic or fruitful; they all become a part of you. They all remain with you until the day you die.

There's a reason for this. It's because at one point in time, you both shared a close connection. And not just any connection, but the most special type of connection in all the universe

Just think about it...are there any exes who still cross your mind? Don't worry, you're not alone in this. You're not crazy or obsessive. I also think of my exes from time to time. Nothing crazy or outlandish, but sometimes I wonder how they're doing. It's quite normal to have these thoughts. And with all the social media platforms in our society, it's almost impossible not to bump into a few of them. But be careful, because a lot of people aren't too fond of their significant other being cool with an ex. I personally have never had a problem with any of my girlfriends being cool with an ex. Well, let me explain the difference because there is a difference.

When I say cool with an ex, I'm not talking about "buddy-buddy, best-friend" cool. I'm talking about acquaintance cool. There are exes who are buddy-buddy close and have never dared to cross any unfavorable lines. It always boils down to respecting your partner's comfort with the ex. I have three exes who always keep in touch with me, and none of us find this to be uncomfortable or weird. Two of them have been in my life for twenty years (since I was an adolescent), while another has been present for well over ten years.

All of us live in different parts of the U.S., which makes our communication a lot easier. If anyone of them live up the street or were physically present every day, things would be uncomfortable. Not because we would be secretly be trying to get with one another, but because our physical presence would put added pressure on our current relationships. Think about it...what if you saw your girlfriend's ex every day? What if he and your girlfriend had a friendly relationship? Sure, you might be saying, "Wouldn't have a problem with it. I trust her." And right now, you might, but what about in three months or six months? What about when the fights and arguments come? The human mind is a powerful tool, and sometimes it can be a deceptive one. With time, our insecurities, doubts, and experiences from past toxic relationships might get the best of you.

So, now imagine if the shoe was on the other foot and it was your girlfriend dealing with the close proximity of her ex. This is why if you're friends with an ex, you'll always need to be mindful and respectful of your significant other's feelings. Yes, I and some of my exes communicate as friends, but always with respect toward our partners. One of my exes and I are so open and honest about our friendship, her significant other and I have communicated on many occasions. We've talked about everything, and I remember they were going through a rough time. They were having complications with conceiving, which put a big strain on the relationship. It honestly felt rewarding to be a friend to her and her husband when they needed it.

This is what I think a ex is about—it's about maturing and understanding that just because you may have not been the best boyfriend she needed doesn't mean you can't be the best friend she needs. I take pride in being someone's ex. I feel like if I was ever in a relationship with you, then you were a pretty special person. There was something unique about you. That's the power of love; there's no on or off switch. Even though you aren't in love with them anymore, you may still have some love for them. You still want to see them live a happy, joyous, and successful life.

Now, some of you may be reading this and scratching your heads. If you're having a hard time understanding this, it's probably for two reasons. One, you're probably still in love with your ex and have never fully received closure. Or two, your past relationship was toxic and all you have for this particular ex is hard feelings. There will always be the exes that we're cool with and the ones that we'll never be cool with. Even though I've dated plenty of women, only three remain. Not as reminders of what could've been, but as reminders of what good friends are.

Long gone are the days when we were madly in love with each other. We've all matured and moved on with our lives, but our true unselfish connection still remains. Them being in my life has become so normal, sometimes I forget that we once dated. It feels like being in cruise control. There's no uneasy feelings or any underlying motives.

Whenever we communicate, it's genuine. This can be very complicated to explain to others. And from my understanding, there are three reasons why.

One, they don't see love and sexual desire as two different things. In their mind, if you have love for them (and are not in love with them), then you must still have a sexual desire for them. Two, they don't believe that the male and female gender can coexist in a non-intimate relationship; simply put, men and women can't be friends. Three, they are victims of liars and cheaters, and suffer from trust issues. All of these things can not only make being friends with the opposite gender complicated, but make being friends with your ex seem impossible.

So don't take it personally if your current lover feels a certain way about your relationship with your past lover. Remember to be understanding and respectful. You might just have to limit the communication between you and your ex for a while. Don't worry, though, because if it's a genuine friendship, your ex will be understanding and considerate of your new love life. And maybe with time, your current partner will understand that her position is in no way in jeopardy and begin to understand the bond you and your ex share.

CHAPTER 12

Commitment

(Never be afraid to fall or give it your all)

As men, some of us grew up being taught things that weren't totally true. Some of us were taught that men don't cry or show emotion. That men shouldn't be afraid of or dependent on others.

All of these teachings have handicapped us when it comes to relationships. A relationship is a living thing. It is forever shape-shifting and transforming. There isn't an equation or blueprint to it. There isn't any specific set of rules or guidelines, either. A relationship is forever evolving.

A lot of men take pride in having control. Usually, when you control a situation, you can sometimes know the outcome. If you know the outcome of a situation, you'll have no fear or anxiety. Fear and anxiety come from not knowing. Some of us put on this big front and act like we aren't surprised when things don't go our way. Like we planned it or we evaluated every possible outcome. This is why being fully committed to a relationship is complicated for us.

Think about it...let's say you work at a job where you can climb up the ladder, and you aspire to become the CEO. You've done the math and figure it'll take you fifteen years to accomplish this goal. You know the obstacles that can get in the way of your goal, so you adjust accordingly. Each and every day, you show up to work energized and positive. You give every day all your energy. You are set on your goal of becoming the CEO.

But what if you knew that no matter how hard you worked, you'd never become CEO? Would you still put in the same amount of energy and effort at work? EXACTLY!

The same principle is true for relationships. The fear of uncertainty makes us uncomfortable. And we, as men, tend to run away from uncomfortable instead of opening up to it. That's because we are taught from a young age to suppress our emotions and feelings. To toughen up.

We embrace and embody this tough guy act. We forget that a relationship between two people is symbiotic. In order to survive, it takes the two. By shutting down and not voicing our feelings and emotions, we appear to be insensitive. It appears as if we don't want or need our partner's help. This is damaging to a life, the feeling of not being wanted or needed.

Our uncertainty in the longevity of a relationship prevents us from giving it our all. Fear is detectable, like some black hole sucking the life out of your relationship. If you show doubt or fear in the relationship, what do you think your partner's going to start doing? If your energy's off, then hers will be also. I'm a big fan of energy and balance in any relationship.

We, as men, have to learn that there are some things that are out of our control. Who our children will be...what others think of us...and most importantly, our women! We have to learn how to accept the things we cannot change and pray to GOD for the guidance and strength to change the things we can. We have to remember that love is a journey. Yes, there will be heartbreaks. Yes, there will be times when you feel like dying and blowing up the world. Yes, there will be times when you feel used and abused. And yes, there will even be times when you second-guess yourself and feel as though you are better off alone. But don't give up, because the rain doesn't last forever.

There will also be wonderful times. Times when you feel so alive. Times you wished you could bottle up the feeling and sell it. Times when no matter how hard, dark, or uncertain the situation, you'll look into your lover's eyes and feel hope that everything will be okay. It is during times like these when you'll be able to say, with utmost certainty, that, "It is better to have loved and lost, then to not have loved at all."

Made in the USA
Coppell, TX
27 July 2025